T0072326

"Few things can paralyze our progress in life like stress, tension and anxiety. Meditations for the Mind-Body-Spirit offers practical meditations to help anyone develop healthier mindsets. This is a succinct, helpful step-by-step guide to helping you let go of your concerns and focus on finding your best self."
Adrian Gostick, New York Times bestselling author of "Anxiety at Work" and "Leading with Gratitude"

"This inspirational book delivers messages of healing, awareness, and well-being. It is a valuable guide that will enable you to find balance and wellness through conscious awareness. As you read these meditations, you'll see that they'll make the journey of your life much more meaningful."
Vincent Bonadies, MS, CTRS- Chief of Recreational Therapy at U.S. Department of Veterans Affairs

"As a current Instructor of Therapeutic Recreation and a former practitioner, I just wish I had this book at my disposal during my days in the field. The meditations are clear, concise, and totally immersive to say the least. I will be using this book in my personal life as well as sharing this with my students as a wonderful reminder of how meditation can be an integral part of our path to wellness!"
Kris Brashner, MA, CTRS, Instructor in Health, Science and Recreation Management, University of Mississippi

"What a great resource! This book contains a variety of ready to use stress relief exercises that will work with a variety of populations and treatment settings."
Jim Fitzgerald, LRT/CTRS Recreational Therapy Supervisor, DSOHF, R.J. Blackley Center–North Carolina Department of Health and Human Services

"Loved it! This book has opened my eyes to the benefits and importance of meditation. I always had an interest but feared it would be too difficult or take too long to learn. After reading this book, I discovered that I can reap huge benefits from even small increments of time. Diane's clear suggestions and techniques are much needed and appreciated tools I will apply on a regular basis. These meditations truly promote a mind, body, and spiritual connection. You will feel lighter, more calm–gaining clarity and optimism to better handle the stressors in your life."
Gina Panzino Lyman- author, Book Reviewer, Podcaster

"Reading through– *Meditations for the Mind-Body-Spirit* was an overwhelming, calming experience in–itself. Diane really captures the beauty and importance of meditation. Each meditation she describes in the book, I could feel and imagine as I read on. This book is very beautifully written. Well done."
Kate Curit, author, Turner Publishing Inc.

Meditations *for the* Mind-Body-Spirit

Audio Book Link included-

Diane Kurtz Calabrese

BALBOA.PRESS
A DIVISION OF HAY HOUSE

Balboa Press books may be ordered through booksellers or by contacting:

Balboa Press
A Division of Hay House
1663 Liberty Drive
Bloomington, IN 47403
www.balboapress.com
844-682-1282

Because of the dynamic nature of the Internet, any web addresses or links contained in this book may have changed since publication and may no longer be valid. The views expressed in this work are solely those of the author and do not necessarily reflect the views of the publisher, and the publisher hereby disclaims any responsibility for them.

The author of this book does not dispense medical advice or prescribe the use of any technique as a form of treatment for physical, emotional, or medical problems without the advice of a physician, either directly or indirectly. The intent of the author is only to offer information of a general nature to help you in your quest for emotional and spiritual well-being. In the event you use any of the information in this book for yourself, which is your constitutional right, the author and the publisher assume no responsibility for your actions.

Any people depicted in stock imagery provided by Getty Images are models, and such images are being used for illustrative purposes only. Certain stock imagery © Getty Images.

Print information available on the last page.

ISBN: 979-8-7652-2646-9 (sc)
ISBN: 979-8-7652-2645-2 (hc)
ISBN: 979-8-7652-2647-6 (e)

Library of Congress Control Number: 2022905858

Balboa Press rev. date: 04/06/2022

Contents

Audiobook link (last page)

Introduction

It is only possible to live happily ever after on a day-to-day basis.
–Margaret Bonnano

This book offers a variety of meditations to enable one to release their daily stress, built up tension, and toxic energy. Guided meditations are a way to let go of your worries for the moment and bring you back to your true, authentic self. It helps re-align the chakras of your body to their natural state of vibration, –where you can live more fully, love more abundantly, and react in a peaceful state of mind. Your mind, body, and spirit are the essential parts of you. You are God's precious gift to the world and there is nothing more beautiful than a soul in the state of peace.

As I wrote in my previous book, –Mind, Body, Spirit and Discovering the Purpose of Life, –guided meditation is one of many holistic healing modalities that has many benefits. The practice of guided meditation is dated back to the beginning of time. We all need to quiet the mind, to let go of all the chatter of everyday life, –to recharge, replenish and rejuvenate the soul.

Meditation can be implemented for long and short periods of time. We live in a world that is constantly cluttering our lives. We need to take time out for ourselves. When we do that, –we feel more relaxed. We can give more of ourselves and to others in positive ways because we are refreshed. Meditation lifts our spirit to a higher level of vibration so that we can handle life's troubles and triumphs to our best capability.

While working at the Veteran's Administration Medical Center in Northport, Long Island, –I would always include guided meditations as part of my practice with my patients. Many patients felt the soothing music and aromatherapy used in conjunction with the guided meditations made the experience even more pleasant, so it's important to take note of what works best for you. There's always something you can add or take away from the practice to make it more suited for you. The most important step is taking the leap to improve your overall health and wellness, –taking time out for "you."

This book is in dedication to Jesus Christ,
our eternal begotten father, Creator
of all that is and ever will be.

With a special thank you to my husband
and children who have supported me in
my career and with my publications.

A special appreciation and gratitude
to all the patients I have worked with
over the years, -I learned from you as
much as you learned from me.

Special thanks to David Dachinger, from
Loving Meditations, --who did a wonderful
job recording and editing my audiobook.

Special thanks to the artists from Pixabay
for free copyright images and music
to enhance the audiobook, -especially
NaturesEYE, REDproductions, SerErmoloff,
PalboGaez, Patrizio, Madirfan,
ZakharValaha, and Adi Goldstein.

Special thank you to all who have
volunteered their time to review my book, -
for their support and beautiful words.

And a special devotion to all those who read
or will listen to this book; may God bless over
you always and guide you on your journey
of life and through your healing process.

1

Getting Started with Meditation

Meditation is waiting on God.
-Mahatma Gandhi

Meditation is a practice known to man since the beginning of time. The history of meditation is rooted back in religion and spiritual practice; however, as cultures and societies changed, −so did its practice. The English word "meditation" comes from *meditatum*, a Latin word meaning to "ponder." When we ponder, −we reflect, we think. But instead of thinking in haste, −we think with clarity. We let go of toxic thoughts, −calming the mind, body, and soul to lead a more peaceful and happy life.

There are many benefits to prayer, meditation, and guided imaginary. As I talked about in my previous book, −Mind, Body, Spirit and Discovering the Purpose of Life, −meditation has proven benefits to reduce anxiety and depression; fear and apprehension; stress and tension; calming your mind and nerves; and improving your physical health.

There are various forms of meditation and differences in how people respond to meditation. Each time you practice meditation, −you are generally, −able to let go more easily, and may go into a deeper meditation with each experience. You become light itself. Meditation increases your concentration and ability to stay focused. And it ultimately increases your wisdom and intuition.

Meditating in the morning provides you with inspirational energy for the day, –and meditating in the evening encourages a restful sleep.

There are many ways to meditate. In the next chapters I will go into short and long meditations providing various guided imageries to engage your mind, body, and spirit into a state of relaxation. Everyone has a different point of view on what helps them to relax, –so that is why I provide a variety of meditations to choose from. Some of my patients in the past enjoyed short meditations, others enjoyed breathing exercises, –while others enjoyed guided imageries. Remember there is no right or wrong way to meditate, –as long as it provides you with a positive experience that fosters relaxation to your mind, body, and spirit.

Try not to get frustrated with the practice of meditation as it takes time to become comfortable with the technique. Be patient with yourself. There are different stages to meditation.

The *first stage* is simply to ignore thought. We always have distracting thoughts on our minds, –when that happens, just bring yourself back to a state of peace.

The *second stage* is to be able to stop thoughts successfully for longer periods of time, –moving your awareness beyond the awareness of this world.

In the *third stage* of meditation, –you have no thoughts. You have reached a higher level of meditation in that you are on a different plane. Some people who have reached this level claim that had an out-of-body experience, –where they felt as if they were floating around the room, –or were somewhere else for some time, –or where their mind and spirit drifted.

You must remember there is nothing to be afraid of in meditation. You are allowing your body to rest, —and your spirit to feel a euphoric feeling of deep relaxation.

This state of calmness is often hard to achieve as a beginner. Many people who have practiced meditation for years do not reach that state, —so don't put pressure on yourself. Even if the practice of meditation helps to provide a sense of *calm* for only a brief period of time, —it's still worthwhile. It is truly an accomplishment and a reward worth achieving and receiving.

To reiterate from my previous book, —Mind, Body, Spirit and Discovering the Purpose of Life, —every thought begins with an *intention*, and that intention leads to an *action,* —so if you have positive thoughts that the meditation will work, —it most likely will.

Prior to starting your meditation, —set an intention for *healing.*

Find a quiet comfortable place that is dimly lit, —where you will be undistracted for five to fifteen minutes, or —however long you want to meditate for.

You may use an audio-guided meditation, —or choose to quietly meditate on your own.

If you choose to meditate on your own, —put on soothing music or nature sounds.

You may also want to add aromatherapy by diffusing a particular essential oil or blend during the meditation.

Sit in a comfortable chair with your feet flat on floor or sit on the floor in a cross-legged seat.

Relax your shoulders, —keep your palms facing up for more receptivity or keep your palms down for more grounding.

Then close your eyes, —and start your meditation practice.

2

Breath Meditations

Be Still and Breathe.
–Ivoryline

One of the simplest meditations is to focus your attention on your breath. It's an "entry level" meditation anyone can do. It provides an immediate sense of relaxation that helps to enhance your overall health. It helps to reduce anxiety and fear, it helps to restore a sense of calm, and it helps to shift your mood with a fresh start for the day.

Take between five and fifteen minutes to try this short breath meditation:

Get comfortable in a chair or cross-legged seat on the floor.
If in a chair, –keep your feet flat on the floor for grounding.

Place your palms facing down on your lap
or over your belly, –one above the other.
Close your eyes.

Inhale- slowly through your nose.
Exhale- slowly through your mouth.

Continue- to inhale slowly.
And- to exhale slowly.

Stay focused on your breathing.
If you have any distracting thoughts, —
release them to God or the universe.

Re-focus yourself on your breath
and the rising and falling of your belly.

Try holding your breath for a second or two, —
then release any residual tension in your body.

Repeat one or two more times, —
and when you are ready, —
come back to the present time, —
and open your eyes.

Take inventory of the breath meditation:

How did this meditation work for you?

Is there something you could add or take away from this meditation to make it more comfortable for you?

Do you think a longer version would be better?

Now try an optional- longer version of the breath meditation.

Find a quiet place to take fifteen to thirty minutes for this meditation.

Again, —sit in a comfortable chair or in a cross-legged seat.
If in a chair, —keep your feet flat on the floor for grounding.

Place your palms facing down on your lap
or over your belly, —one above the other.
Close your eyes.

Breathe in through your nose.
Exhale through your mouth.

Start off with slow breaths.

Then gradually inhale and exhale, —using normal breathing.

As you inhale, —imagine breathing in crisp fresh spring air.
As you exhale, —imagine releasing all negative
energies that have been weighing you down.

Continue focusing on your breath.

If you experience any distracting thoughts, —
release them to God or the universe.

Note how replenishing it is to release all your
stored up toxic energy to the universe.

Feel yourself become lighter with each breath.

Note how your body begins to relax with each exhalation.

With each new inhalation, —welcome positive
energy to rejuvenate your spirit.

With each exhalation, —let go of anything
weighing on your mind and body.

Take deeper breaths in.
Hold them for a second before releasing, —
and exhale slowly.

Feel the light of the God healing you.
Focus on your unique gifts God has given you with each breath in.
Releasing any negative thoughts with each breath out.

Remember you are never alone in the universe.
God, —is always with you.

Take another deep breath in.
Exhale with a slight smile.

When you are ready, —return to the present time,
and —open your eyes.

Take inventory of this longer breath meditation:

Do you feel more relaxation or energized?

Did this meditation work for you?

Is there something you could add *or* take away from this meditation experience to make it better?

What did you like better, —the shorter or longer version of the meditation?

3

Mantra Meditations

*Only when we are no longer
afraid, do we begin to live.
–Dorothy Thompson*

Mantra meditations are meditations to inspire you to set affirmations. They cleanse your spirit and refresh you by, –bringing in positive energy into your heart and soul. They also provide an immediate sense of relaxation to help your overall health for short and longer periods of time if done regularly.

Take between five and fifteen minutes to try the "Let it go to God" meditation.

*Sit in a comfortable chair or in a cross-legged seat.
If in a chair, –keep your feet flat on the floor for grounding.
Place your palms facing down on your lap or
place your palms facing up for more receptivity.
Relax your shoulders.
Close your eyes or lower your eyes to the ground.
You may alternatively, –keep your eyes open, and –focus
on a lava lamp or other sensory item instead.*

I am going to ask you to say a five-word phrase over and over
in your mind.

"Let it go to God" or if you prefer, say—
"Let it go to the universe."

You may link these five words to your breathing
or not link it at all.
Find the way you like best.

Continue to repeat your five-word phrases in your mind.

Focus only on those words.
If you become distracted, —redirect your thoughts to those words.

As you say these five words, —release anything in
your mind that is causing you distress.

Trust that God is watching over for you.
Have faith that the universe is working it all out.
Repeat your five-word phrase, —
until you begin to feel light again.

Now let go of this technique and notice how you are feeling.

When you are ready, —take a deep breath in.
Exhale slowly, —
and open your eyes.

Take inventory of this mantra meditation:

Do you feel more relaxation or energized?

Take note if repeating phases in your mind helps you? —Perhaps a
different phase would help you.

Would a longer version of this meditation be better?

Now try an optional–longer version of a mantra meditation.

Find a quiet place to take fifteen to thirty minutes for this meditation.

This time we will work through areas of emotional and physical distress by repeating the words "Let it go" in your mind.

Again, –sit in a comfortable chair or in a cross-legged seat.
If in a chair, –keep your feet flat on the floor for grounding.
Place your palms facing down on your lap or
place your palms facing up for more receptivity.
Relax your shoulders.
Close your eyes or lower your eyes to the ground.
Another option is to keep your eyes open, –focusing
on a lava lamp or other sensory item.

I am going to ask you to say this three-word phrase in your mind, –
"Let it go."
After each affirmation is stated, –release each feeling
to God and the universe.
Then repeat silently, – "Let it go."

I want you to imagine God and the universe working
cooperatively to rid all feelings of loneliness away.

I want you to imagine God and the universe working
cooperatively to rid all feelings of anxiety away.

I want you to imagine God and the universe working
cooperatively to rid all feelings of sadness and loss away.

I want you to imagine God and the universe working
cooperatively to rid all feelings of judgement away.

I want you to imagine God and the universe working
cooperatively to rid all feelings of jealously away.

I want you to imagine God and the universe working
cooperatively to rid all feelings of fear away.

I want you to imagine God and the universe working
cooperatively to rid all feelings of fatigue away.

I want you to imagine God and the universe working
cooperatively to rid all feelings of pain and hurt away.

Now take a deep breath in, —exhale slowly.
Repeat one to two more times.

Notice how light you are beginning to feel.
You now have the weight of the world lifted from you.

Be assured you are not alone in this universe.
God is always with you.
Remember, —to always ask God to help you.

When you are ready, —come back to the room.
And —open your eyes.

Taking inventory of this mantra meditation:

Do you feel more relaxed and re-energized?

Did this longer version of the meditation work for you?

Is there something you could add or take away from this meditation to make you more comfortable?

Always have awareness of what works best for you going forward.

Diane Kurtz Calabrese

4

Chakra Alignment Meditation

You are the light of the world.
–Matthew 5:14-16

The chakra alignment meditation focuses on the seven chakras of the body and the colors associated with each chakra. The color of the light changes as it descends from your crown chakra all the way to the root chakra. It helps bring peace and tranquility into your mind-body-spirit. It provides an immediate sense of relaxation and restoration within your body that transcends your overall health and wellness, –as it realigns the energy centers of your body. Take your time with this meditation, –go at your own pace releasing any toxins from each chakra area that is not serving your highest good.

Take fifteen to thirty minutes to try this meditation:

Sit in a comfortable chair or in a cross-legged seat.
If in a chair, –keep your feet flat on the floor for grounding.
Place your palms facing down on your lap or
place your palms facing up for more receptivity.
Relax your shoulders.
Close your eyes or lower your eyes to the ground.

Another option is to keep your eyes open, —focusing
on a lava lamp or other sensory item.

Starting from the crown chakra, —imagine a white celestial light
flowing in through your crown chakra-on top of your head.

Gently breathe in this light.
Exhale—spreading this light throughout the top or crown part
of your head, —bringing clarity to your mind, —and
enveloping you with wisdom and connection to the divinity.

Continue breathing in-light.
Then gently, exhale—spreading the light.

Now, inhale the light, —releasing it to the next chakra, —
the third eye or brow chakra.

Notice how the light changes from white to lavender, —
reflective of the color of the chakra.
Imagine the light taking away any physical or emotional pain in
your head, —replenishing it with inspiration and knowledge.

Breathe in the lavender light.
Exhale, and—spread the lavender light across your third eye, and—
lower parts of your face and head.

Continue to gently breathe there for a moment.

Then take a deep breath in, —release the light into your throat chakra.

Notice how the light changes from lavender to blue in color.

Continue to gently breathe in here.
Exhale—spreading this blue light throughout your neck and shoulders, —
releasing any residual pain or tension in your neck, —and
fostering truth and communication.

Continue to gently breathe there for a moment.

Then take a deep breath in, —releasing the light into your heart chakra.

Observe how the light changes from blue to green in color.

Continue to breathe gently.
Spread the green light throughout your chest
cavity, your arms and into your lungs.

Notice yourself become filled with the warm love of God.
You're becoming one with the light.

Continue to gently breathe there for a moment.

Notice how your body expels residual pain or emotions
that have been blocking your heart or lung area.

Take a deep breath in —and release the light into your
solar-plexus chakra.

Observe how the light changes from green to yellow in color.

Continue to breathe gently, —spreading this yellow light throughout
your abdomen, —taking away all your worries, and
restoring your self-confidence.

Continue to gently breathe there for a moment.

Now take a deep breath in and—release the light into your
naval chakra.

Observe how the light changes from yellow to orange in color.

Continue to breathe gently, —spreading this orange light throughout
your naval area, lower intestines, and reproductive organs.

You are now becoming very relaxed and sensual.
Notice how you have a greater capacity to express emotion.

Continue to gently breathe there for a moment.

Take a deep breath in, —releasing the light into your root chakra.

Observe the light changing from orange to red in color. You are becoming more grounded now.

Continue to breathe gently, —spreading this red light throughout your pelvic area and lower extremities.

Notice how this red light is helping to release any pain you may have been experiencing in the joints of your hips, legs, knees, ankles, or feet.

You are now feeling stronger, more vibrant, and ready to take on the world again.

Take another deep breath in. Exhale slowly and—open your eyes.

Taking inventory of the chakra alignment meditation:

Do your energy centers feel more aligned?

Do you feel more energized?

Did visualizing the colors of the chakra centers help through the process of chakra realignment?

Is there something you could add or take away from this meditation experience that would make it more comfortable for you?

Would a longer or shorter version of this meditation work better?

These are but a few questions to contemplate going forward.

5

Body-Part & Pain-Release Meditation

However vast the darkness, we
must supply our own light.
-Stanley Kubrick

The purpose of this meditation is to distract you from any specific pain that you are experiencing in one or more parts of your body. It could be an emotional or physical pain. It also helps to keep your mind focused on a given area of your body to demonstrate appreciation for your body temple and how you can heal yourself with your thoughts.

Take fifteen to thirty minutes to try this meditation:

Sit in a comfortable chair or in a cross-legged seat.
If in a chair, —keep your feet flat on the floor for grounding.
Place your palms facing down on your lap or
place your palms facing up for more receptivity.
Relax your shoulders.
Close your eyes or lower your eyes to the ground.
Another option is to keep your eyes open, —focusing
on a lava lamp or other sensory item.

Starting from the root chakra, —focus your attention on your feet.
Then — to your ankles.
Now move your attention to your shins.
From your shins move your attention to your knees.
Now move your attention to your thighs.
Then move your attention to your hips and pelvic area.

Now move your attention to your naval chakra
area, —below your belly button.
Focus on your lower back.
Then move your attention to your lower abdomen.

Now move your attention to your solar plexus area.
Focus on your stomach, —your upper abdomen.
Gently breathe there.

Then move your attention to your heart chakra, —your chest cavity.
Focus on your lungs, and—breathe here.
Focus on your upper back and spinal region.

Move your attention to your right and left shoulders.
Focus your attention on the space between your shoulders and elbows.
Now focus on the space between your elbows and hands.
Focus on your hands and fingers.

Now turn your attention to your throat
chakra, —the areas all around your neck.
Focus on the front of your neck.
Now the back of your neck.

Now move your attention to your third eye/brow chakra.
Focus your attention on your face.
Then —on your mouth.
Now your nose.
And- your eyes.

Now focus your attention on your cheeks.
Now your ears.
Now on your eyebrows and forehead.
Now the back of your head.

Now turn your attention to your crown chakra, —the top of your head.
Notice any sensations when you breathe there.

Now slowly begin to descend your awareness downward.
Guiding your attention slowly, —at your own pace.
Allow yourself to let go of all unhealthy toxins in your body.
Understand that God and the universe are restoring
your body to its natural healthy state.

Take a deep breath in.
Exhale, —slowly and
open your eyes.

An option when implementing this meditation is to incorporate self-healing reiki hand placements. I have often observed my patients do this as they claimed it helped them to focus their attention on each body part, —which enhanced the healing effect of the meditation.

Take inventory of the body-part & pain-release meditation:

How did this meditation work for you?

What changes would you make going forward?

Remember there is no right or wrong with meditation, —it's an individual practice—servicing your highest good.

Diane Kurtz Calabrese

6

Sensory Meditation

Your life is your magical wand.
–Mike Dooley

The sensory meditation focuses on our six senses including our sixth sense, –which is our natural intuition–our sense of knowing. It helps to relax your mind-body-spirit by bringing you into an escaped world, –fostering peace and tranquility through imagination. Take your time with this meditation. Allow yourself to have the full benefit of each sense in this experience. If negative thoughts enter your mind, –just release them to God–for they will not serve your highest good. Remember to put on soothing music, diffuse essential oils, or use any other sensory items to enhance the experience before you start.

Take fifteen to thirty minutes to try this meditation:

Sit in a comfortable chair.
Keep your feet flat on the floor for grounding.
Place your palms facing down on your lap.
Relax your shoulders.
Close your eyes.

Allow yourself to go to a place in nature that is serene and peaceful.
It could be a place you've visited before or
a place that you are imagining.

Wherever you are, —make yourself comfortable, —
as if there were no time at all.

Breathe gently here.

Feel yourself just in flow with this place, —for you it is your paradise.

Notice any sounds you hear from this place.
It could be a gentle breeze, birds chirping, or water sounds, —
whatever it is—make it soothing to you.
Take your time processing all these sounds.

Next, observe what you are feeling.
Is there anything that you want to pick up, and hold or touch?
Notice how this substance feels.

Be in tune to your body parts, —and the climate you are in.

Do you want to sit and rest where you are for a while or —do you feel-
like running, jumping, or rolling on whatever surface you are on?
Do—what feels natural to you.

Stay in that moment for a few more breaths.

Now observe what you are seeing.
What things in nature are in your paradise?
Are you with any people or animals?
What are you most mesmerized by?

Observe any tastes in your mouth from the environment you're in.
Are these tastes pleasant?
If not, —refocus your attention on a pleasant taste you'd like to invite in.

Observe any distinct aromas such as flowers.
Invite in favorite aromas that you enjoy smelling.

Take your time investigating this timeless place.

Now I'd like you to use your sixth sense.
Feel free to invite in someone you can't necessarily
see or feel, —but know they are there.
It could be a special person, guide, angel, or animal.
Whoever it is—know that they are making this
place even more magnificent for you.

Imagine a special message that they are telling you that gives
you reassurance that you are truly loved and protected.

Now, —imagine getting a warm hug from whomever you invited in.
Be rest assured you will see them again.

Take a moment to take in a deep breath in.
Offer gratitude for this experience.

Exhale slowly, —returning to the present time.
And—open your eyes.

This is a beautiful meditation because it invites in your own personal insights. Through your imagination, —you can relax in a place that means serenity to you.

Take inventory of the sensory meditation:

Note how did this meditation work for you?

Would you make any changes next time?

Is there anything you would add or take away from this meditation experience?

7

Seashore Meditation

*One should lie empty, open, choiceless as a
beach-waiting for a gift from the sea.*
-Anne Morrow Lindbergh

The seashore meditation brings you to a place in nature using your imagination at a shoreline. The beach is a place to calm the mind, as well as to restore peace and tranquility into your body and spirit. Be observant in this meditation, —notice the little things that offer inspiration and joy. You may want to put on sounds of ocean waves, or other soothing music during this meditation to help enhance the mood.

Take fifteen to thirty minutes to enjoy this meditation:

Sit in a comfortable chair or in a cross-legged seat.
Keep your feet flat on the floor for grounding.
Place your palms facing down on your lap.
Relax your shoulders.
Close your eyes.

Take a deep breath in—through your nose.
Exhale—slowly through your mouth.
Observe yourself sitting on a beach chair.

Your feet are nestled in the warm sand.

Feel the warmth of the sun reflecting off your face and body.

*As you look around imagine that this is the most
beautiful beach you've ever seen.*

*As you look up you see the most beautiful white seagulls, –
flying in the sky.
They are so graceful and beautiful, –with a twinkle in their eye.
You feel like they are sending loving messages as they fly over you.*

They are pure white and look like heavenly doves.

*As you sit in your chair, –imagine your fingers combing the sand.
Note how the sand feels in your hands.*

*Imagine discovering the most beautiful seashell.
Take note of what it looks like.
And –put it in your pocket.*

*Take another deep breath in, –through your nose.
Exhale–appreciating all that you see.*

*Now imagine yourself getting out of the beach
chair to take a walk along the shore.*

*You feel the water from the ocean touch your feet.
Imagine that it is the most perfect temperature.*

Notice how tranquilizing it is to watch the waves.

*As the waves roll in, –imagine new inspiration coming your way.
And–as the waves roll out, –
imagine letting go of any residual energy that is holding you back.*

Take a few moments here to decide whether you
want to take a swim in the water or
if you'd like to continue watching the waves by the shore.

Concentrate on the sounds of the waves.
And—allow your body and spirit to be in sync with its rhythm.
Notice tropical fish swimming peacefully by you.
Be rest assured that all marine life is in perfect harmony with you.

Notice a dolphin in the distance swimming with his mate.
Observe how graceful they are together.

Feel a great sense of peace and tranquility here.

Now imagine yourself walking back to your beach chair.
Feel the warm sun dry you right up.
Feel completely content here.

Now imagine a warm breeze pass as you sit back in your chair.

Notice how much more energized you feel being in nature.

At this moment—feel free to invite in another person
or animal to be with you at this beach.

Observe what you are doing together.

Note the joy you are giving and receiving at this magnificent seashore.
Smile here.
Take a deep breath in through your nose.
Exhale slowly through your mouth and
know that you can return to this place anytime you wish.
With another deep breath in, exhaling slowly—
return to the present time.
And—open your eyes.

This is a serene meditation used to provide peace and tranquility into your life. If you are not a fan of the beach you can always substitute the beach with another waterway that is inviting to you.

Take inventory of the seashore meditation:

How did this meditation work for you?

Take note of what works or doesn't work for you in your meditation practice.

What changes or enhancers would you use going forward?

8

Rainforest Meditation

The love of all living creatures is the
most noble attribute of man.
-Charles Darwin

The rainforest meditation offers mystery and adventure to relax the mind, —fostering inspiration. Keep in mind, nature meditations are meant to restore harmony and peace within your spirit. They renew your sense of hope, peace, tranquility, and zest for life. Using your imagination to *calm* your mind-body-spirit. Be observant in this meditation, —notice all things that offer inspiration and joy to your life. You may want to put on soothing nature sounds during this meditation to help enhance the mood as well as diffuse aromatherapy oils.

Take fifteen to thirty minutes to enjoy this meditation:

Sit in a comfortable chair.
Keep your feet flat on the floor for grounding.
Place your palms facing down on your lap or
up for more receptivity.
Relax your shoulders.
Close your eyes.
Take a deep breath in.

Exhale slowly.

Imagine yourself walking through a beautiful, peaceful rainforest, —knowing there is nothing in this rainforest that can hurt you.

You are on a journey to discover the love of nature.

As you enter the rainforest note any sounds you may hear.

While you're walking down the path of the woods, —notice a beautiful red hummingbird fly in front of you. The hummingbird lands on a nearby tree branch. You stop and look at the bird. Notice how his eyes twinkle with joy as the bird looks back at you.

You continue walking down the wooded path and hear a waterfall not too far away. The sound of the water gets louder as you come closer. You turn the corner of the path, and in the distance—you see a deer and her calf drinking from the waterfall. You stop and just observe the doe and her calf for a few moments, —just peacefully watching them.

You then see a rabbit and her bunnies hop over to the waterfall. The animals are peaceful and loving toward one another.

As you walk further into the rainforest you see elephants in the jungle, — peacefully mingling with their babies.

They gaze over your way with a twinkle in their eye, — knowing you are enjoying their company.

The baby elephants dance around with one another, —as children would in a park. They are so delightful to watch.

You walk further into the rainforest and notice how tall the trees are.
The leaves on the trees are a beautiful shade
of green, —its aura is so serene.

Everything looks so healthy and lively.

You look down and see beautiful daisies swaying in the wind.
They are a bright yellow, —reflective of love and happiness.
The color seems to shine so brightly with the sun's reflection.
You walk over to the daisy and pick it up to smell it.
The pleasant scent engulfs you.

You walk over to a tree stump off the path to sit and rest for a while.
There you delightfully notice two squirrels run by.
They are very friendly and sit by you as you rest on the tree stump.

You are captivated by the auras of the forest, —they are so magnificent.

In the distance you hear gorillas, —they are
peacefully enjoying the beautiful day.
You hear them hitting their chest and chuckling in content.

You get up and walk a little further down the path.

You rest by another nearby waterfall listening to the gorillas'
harmonic sounds.
You have no fear of being harmed by them, —as you
know you are divinely protected on this journey.

The sound of the waterfalls comforts you.
The water looks refreshing.
You decide to splash your face and the water droplets
sparkle with the shimmering sunlight above you.

You feel completely safe and relaxed in this serene place.

Take a moment here—to take in more of this wonderous rainforest.
Imagine what other beautiful scenes in nature you might see.

You are almost near the end of the rainforest now.
At this moment express gratitude for all the encounters
God has shown you along this journey.
You have a deeper sense of connection to these
animals and all that you observed.
You understand they are God's creatures, —and how
gracious they were to welcome you into their home.

You feel light again.
Reenergized with hope with hope of everlasting
peace, hope, and gratitude —for all life.

Take a deep breath in.
Absorb the light of our life force energy.
Exhale—releasing anything that does not serve your highest good.

And—now slowly open your eyes.

This is a good meditation for relaxation and to let go of fear, —putting your faith and trust into the Lord that he will protect you.

Take inventory of the rainforest meditation:

How did this meditation work for you?

Take note of what works or doesn't work for you on your journey to self-discovery.

Remember to add or to take away anything that doesn't serve your highest good.

Note if there are there any changes you would make going forward?

9

Time Capsule Meditation

Be still and know that I am with you.
–Psalm 46:10

The time capsule meditation allows you to go to a time in your life where you felt the most at peace. It enables you to reflect back-in-time where perhaps you felt your spirit was more free, less stressed, or –when you felt the most at ease. If you can't recall a time, use your imagination to visualize what that would look like. Be observant in this meditation. Notice all things that offered you inspiration and joy in that moment. If negative thoughts enter your mind, –quickly release them to God. Feel free to diffuse aromatherapy oils and to put on soothing music to enhance the mood.

Take fifteen to thirty minutes to enjoy this meditation:

Sit in a comfortable chair.
Keep your feet flat on the floor for grounding.
Place your palms facing down on your lap.
Relax your shoulders.
Close your eyes or lower your eyes to the ground.
Take a deep breath in.
Exhale slowly.

*Take a moment to think about a time when
you felt the most at ease in your life.*

*Start by thinking about the age you were most happy.
If you can't, —then create a time in the future to
visualize what that would look like.*

Relive that day like it is happening right now.

Note what season it is, —and the weather.

*Note where you are.
And—who you are with.*

*Reflect on whether you were invited to this place, or
was it spontaneous that you were there?*

Observe what you are wearing, and—if you are holding anything special.

*Ponder upon whether it was the first time you met someone special.
Note if there were any activities going on.*

Were there any aromas in the air?

Was there anything special you were eating or drinking?

How did you feel? Note any feelings sensed by others.

What were you doing that most excited or relaxed you?

Note the level of gratitude for having been there at that time.

Is there anything you would change to enhance that moment?

*Take a deep breath in, —having gratitude for this visit.
Exhale—releasing any regrets.*

Remember you can always revisit this moment again, —anytime you wish.

Your soul is eternal.
Give gratitude to God and the universe for
remembering what happiness looks like.

Know you can create happiness within you.

You are loved more than you will ever know.
Take your time reflecting here, —recognizing what peace looks like.

When you are ready, slowly open your eyes.
And—awaken with a greater sense of knowing that you
can accomplish whatever your heart desires.

This meditation provides hope that whatever you have felt in the past, —can be experienced again. Reminding you that you are the author of your life. Even if that happiness has not been found yet. It is never too late.

As-long-as you are alive, —you get to write your story. When you are on the right path God, and all the universe is behind you. It all comes to intention. Set positive intentions, and —trust, trust that they will unfold to higher expectations than you can ever imagine.

Take inventory of the time capsule meditation:

How did this meditation work for you?

Was this experience something you lived, or—was it something you imagined?

Is there anything you would want to add or to take away from this meditation to make it more comfortable for you next time?

10

Bird's Eye Meditation

*Let us not go back in anger or forward
in fear, but around in awareness.
-James Thurber*

The bird's eye meditation is a wonderful meditation to explore the world from of a different perspective. Discover your sacred place through the eyes of a bird, –offering enrichment, gratitude, and appreciation for all that is around us. Freeing the spirit of unnecessary tension, reducing anxiety and fear, and above all learning to love what we already have.

Take fifteen to thirty minutes to enjoy this meditation:

*Sit in a comfortable chair.
Keeping your feet flat on the floor.
Place your palms facing down next to you or
place your palm up for more receptivity.
Relax your shoulders.
Close your eyes.*

*Take a deep breath in, –absorbing in positive energy.
Exhale–what is not serving your highest good.*

*Imagine you are a bird soaring up into the sky, —gliding
along where the wind carries you.*

*Imagine as you're gliding through the air, —
that you are releasing all toxic energy that has been stored
up inside you.*

*Coordinate soaring through the air with breathing in —
fresh clean positive energy.
And exhale—all that is stressing you.*

*Imagine the heavens taking all that toxic energy
away, —renewing your spirit as you glide through the air.*

*As you venture off, —take note of all that is below you.
Imagine you have the eye of an eagle.
Take in all that is below you.*

*Observe the beautiful evergreen trees in nature.
Notice the beautiful flowers, lively plants, and —
animals seen in the distance.*

*Note what a miracle life really is.
Notice the curvature of the earth.
Notice how everything is divinely connected.*

*Recognize how perfect nature truly is.
Look at the waterways in the distance.*

Have awareness of your geographical location in your vision.

Feel a sense of pride in the planet earth.

Recognize what adversities you have overcome.

*Understand you are in charge of the wonderful
life that has been given to you by God.*

*Take another deep breath in, —offering glory to what you have.
Exhale, —releasing any residual fears or worries of what you don't have.*

Take a moment here to just breathe and listen here.

Note any sounds of nature in your mind as you fly over this region.

*In the distance notice a beautiful mountain top.
Observe its enormous height.
And—below see the depth of the valley.*

*Recognize that all the universe and God are rooting for you
to always succeed.*

*And, when you fly through the valleys of the mountains, —
realize that is where you learned your biggest lessons.*

Without those valleys, —the mountain tops wouldn't be as magnificent.

*Take another deep breath in here.
Exhale slowly.
Understand every adversity offers you deeper wisdom.*

Fly closer to that mountain and imagine yourself landing on the top.

*Feel a sense of joy, gratitude, and patience for all
that you have accomplished thus far in life*

Remember who your greatest teacher is…

*Fold your hands in prayer, —bow to your own heart—namaste.
And—open your eyes.*

The bird's eye meditation restores a sense of peace and tranquility within yourself, –to recognize your accomplishments, to show appreciation for God and all the universe, and to revisit the depths of your struggle, –so you can genuinely appreciate where you are now.

In-order-to set intentions, –we must also recognize what our intentions are, –where we came from, –what we have accomplished thus far.

Remember to always be kind to yourself. You are God's greatest gift, –and are loved more than you know.

Take inventory of the bird's eye meditation:

Did this meditation work for you?

Did you like the idea of soaring through the sky like a bird?

Is there anything you would add or take away from this meditation?

Are there any changes you would want to make going forward?

11

Gratitude Meditation

The art of life is not controlling what happens
to us; but using what happens to us.
–Gloria Steinem

The gratitude meditation offers a period of reflection to appreciate all that you are, –all that you were given, –all that is around you, and –all that you are yet to become. To be appreciated, –we must first appreciate. On this life journey we discover our purpose first by seeing what is already in front of us, –who we are, –what we already have, and –where we are going. The purpose of this meditation is to bring you peace, joy, and contentment for just being alive, –for that alone is a reason to celebrate.

Take fifteen to thirty minutes to enjoy this meditation:

Sit in a comfortable chair.
Keep your feet flat on the floor for grounding.
Place your palms facing down on your lap or
up for more receptivity.
Relax your shoulders.
Close your eyes or lower your eyelids to the ground.

*Take a deep breath in through your nose, —setting
an intention of gratitude.
Exhale through your mouth, —releasing any negative thoughts.*

*Take a few moments to clear your mind of anything
that does not serve your highest good.*

Continue to breathe here.

*Focus your mind on the fact that God gave you life for a purpose.
You don't have think of your purpose, —just
remember you are here for a purpose.*

*Breathe in—appreciation for all life.
Exhale—any doubts of faith and trust to the Lord.*

Affirm in your mind that you are a beautiful soul.

*Breathe in—appreciation for what you have accomplished thus far in life.
Exhale—all regrets or guilt.*

Affirm in your mind the greatest lessons are learned from your mistakes.

*Breathe in—appreciation for those that have supported your efforts.
Exhale—forgiveness for those you haven't.*

Affirm in your mind you—are loved more than you'll ever know.

*Breathe in—appreciation of the beauty of nature.
Exhale—all that is displeasing.*

Affirm in your mind God and the universe are always at work.

*Breathe in—appreciation for your dreams of the future.
Exhale—any demise.*

Affirm "I am"–because I can.
And–recognize with gratitude that you are capable-
of-fulfilling each-and-every dream.

Take one last deep breath in.
Exhale slowly, –and open your eyes.

After this meditation, you should feel stronger and more vibrant, –that you can take on your mission and goals with honor. Have gratitude for all you are, –all you have, –and ever-will-be. It is a state of grace which offers stability and grounding to go forward with your intentions. Showing appreciation for God and all the universe is important. Having gratitude helps to set positive intentions that will make a difference in the outcome of all circumstances. As Gary Zukav once said, "Every action, thought, and feeling is motivated by an intention, and that intention is a cause that exists with one with an effect." In other words, –your intention must be in alignment with the cause, or–it will change the effect.

Take inventory on the gratitude meditation:

Note how well this meditation worked for you.

Note if there is anything you would want to change for next time.

Note if there is anything you would want to add going forward.

12

Heaven's Garden Meditation

God is light, and in him there is no darkness at all.
–John 1:5

Heaven's garden meditation offers a glimpse of heaven through the eyes of those that have either encountered a near-death-experience or had an out-of-body experience. Stories of this have been told throughout the world. In this meditation, I offer an imaginary garden of heaven that fosters hope and serenity to believers and unbelievers alike, –that we are more than just a body, and there is something to look forward to at the end of our lives here on earth. This meditation is used for the purpose of reducing fear and anxiety, decreasing sadness and loneliness as well as the stress of everyday living. Through this guided imagery you will be able to envision what others have seen as-well-as imagine your own visions while walking through this celestial garden.

Make sure you are in a quiet space, in a dimly lit area. Put soft spa music on, keep healing crystals next to you, and diffuse aromatherapy oils if you wish.

Take twenty to thirty minutes to enjoy this meditation:

Sit in a comfortable chair or in a cross-legged seat.
Ground yourself to the floor below you.
Place your palms facing down on your lap or
up for more receptivity.
Relax your shoulders.
Close your eyes.

Take a deep breath in through your nose.
Exhale—slowly through your mouth.

Imagine yourself having the ability to visit heaven's
most magnificent garden, –God's Garden.

You see this beautiful white life-size angel with a
sparking golden halo at your bedside.
You feel this immense love and warm glowing aura around her,
asking you if you'd like to have a glimpse of heaven.

Knowing there is nothing to be afraid of, –
with a warm welcome from this magnificent glowing angel.
The angel takes your hand, and in an instant—you are at
the beginning of the pathway of heaven's garden.

You see beautiful colors in this garden like you've never seen before.
Everything in this garden looks alive, –with the most
immense warmth and compassion for all living things.

As you look down at the ground you see the most dazzling
shade of green grass that you've ever seen. Its aura illuminates
the enormous garden like a sparking emerald.

There are beautiful evergreen trees that compliment
the color of the grass in the distance.
The trees are so large and perfectly trimmed in varying
shades of green color, –it's so sublime and captivating.

You see other trees with various kinds of flowers growing off their branches, —they are equally exquisite in shades of varying colors.

Some of the trees do not look like they are grown on the earth. They are too beautiful for words, and—unfamiliar to the earth.

Under many trees you see beautiful wooden benches, —with craftsmanship like you have never seen before. You walk over to sit down on the bench. You take a moment to take in the beauty of this garden.

The angel sits down beside you and whispers very softly to you in your mind's eye, "What God has instore for you, —you can never even begin to imagine." The angel had a twinkle of delight and a soft smile on her face. She takes immense pride in this heavenly garden and was delighted to show it to you.

As you look out into the garden you see beautiful flowers everywhere, —delightfully swaying in air.

Then you notice the most gorgeous pink roses that your eyes have ever seen. The angel whispers, "It's okay- you can pick one." And—so you do. As you pick up this rose, —you witness another rose immediately grows back to take its place.

It's like magic. Nothing ever dies in this magnificent garden.

You smell the rose, —it has the most wonderful scent. Its scent is so serene and pleasant, not too strong— but long lasting as if you could taste it.

You realize in this garden, —in heaven, you have all your senses and more.

Everything is perfectly placed and tended to
with the utter most care and respect.

The rose brings you an enormous amount of love as
if it were your long-lost love, and soulmate.

Take a few moments here to invite in your own thoughts
of what would also be in this magical garden.

Take a deep breath in.
Exhale slowly.

The angel says, "I'm going to introduce you to
the animals of heaven's garden."
And—you begin to see rabbits, —they are the
purest color white you have ever seen.
Behind them you see reindeer that look like Bambi.

Above you, —you notice white glimmering doves
soaring in the endless shiny blue sky.

Then you see kittens, cats, and dogs of all kinds.
And—a unicorn behind this beautiful evergreen tree.

It is the most beautiful white unicorn you can ever imagine.
It gracefully walks over to you and nods its head.
Telepathically the unicorn sends a loving message
welcoming you to God's Garden.

You feel utterly blessed to have this experience.

The unicorn tells you all of heaven is here waiting for each soul as
they return home, —and you are loved more than you'll ever know.

Inside you feel completely healed by the grace of God.
You have a renewed sense of faith.

And—an overwhelming joy of gratitude.

Suddenly a beautiful lavender and turquoise
colored butterfly lands on your hand.
Its so soft and gentle.
It rests for a moment looking right into your eyes.
Giving you love and reassurance.
Reminding you this is not a dream or fairytale.
Heaven is for real.

The angel whispers in your ear, "It's time to go now."
"This was only a visit."

The angel welcomes you to visit anytime you wish in your dreams.

And—the angel reminds you all of heaven will be here waiting for you
once you have finished all your lessons on the earth.

There is no time in heaven, —so never worry.
Whoever goes before you, will be waiting patiently
on this side as if no time passed at all.

Take a deep breath in.
Know you are protected and cherished by all of heaven.

Exhale slowly, —knowing there is nothing to ever be afraid of.

Then slowly come back to the room and
open your eyes.

At the end of this meditation, allow yourself to feel reassured, hopeful, stronger, and more vibrant. Allow yourself to feel safe and to keep faith and trust in the Lord. Continue to pray and stay focused on positive intentions, —and people that bring you joy, peace, hope and love. You deserve to be happy. All of heaven is rooting for you!

Take inventory of heaven's garden meditation:

Note how well this meditation worked for you.

Note if there is anything you want to add or to take away going forward.

Identify anything you would want to change such as a longer or shorter version of this kind of meditation.

13

Heaven's Gates Meditation

*There is a stream whose runlets gladden the
city of God, the holy dwelling of the most high.
-Psalms 46:5*

Heaven's gates meditation enables you to ponder upon the joyous glory of heaven. Where all of life's answers and our purpose is divinely explained and understood. Step into the faith and trust of God as you explore what awaits us after this experience on the earth plane.

Again, this is a meditation used for the purpose of reducing fear and anxiety, decreasing sadness and loneliness, as-well-as reassuring you of just how loved we all are.

In this guided imagery you will be able to envision what numerous people have claimed to have seen during their NDE, as well as use your own imagination and visions while on a journey walking through the golden gates of heaven.

Make sure you are in a quiet space, –in a dimly lit area. Play soft music with no lyrics. If you wish, keep healing crystals next to you. You may also choose to diffuse aromatherapy oils to enhance the mood.

Take twenty to thirty minutes to enjoy this meditation:

Sit in a comfortable chair or in a cross-legged seat.
Ground yourself to the floor below you.
Place your palms facing down on your lap or
up for more receptivity.
Relax your shoulders.
Close your eyes.

Take a deep breath in through your nose.
Exhale–slowly through your mouth.

As you breathe in, –welcome in a celestial
light from God and the heavens.
Exhale, –all doubt, fear, and destructive thoughts regarding
death and loss.

Continue to breathe gently here.

Begin to understand you are never alone in the universe, –you
are divinely protected by God and the heavenly angels.

Understand that you are a spirit first, –with
a beautiful soul created by God.

You are becoming aware that being on the earth is only a lesson.
Your true home is behind the gates of heaven, –where you came from.

Imagine feeling a sense of unconditional love all around you.

You are beginning to feel the weight and stress
of the earthly world leave you.

Become aware that you will embark on a visit to heaven, –but will
return to earth with a clearer vision of your purpose here on the earth.

You see yourself standing with a beautiful angel, who
has been assigned to you–your entire life.

The angel reassures you that there is nothing to be afraid of.
And you don't only hear it, —you feel it.
You already know it.

You are experiencing instant knowledge of universe.

Things are instantly clear.
There is no need to ask questions because the answers are
coming before the question even needs to be asked.

The gates of heaven begin to open and as you walk
in, —you feel more—and—more love surround you.
There are no words to describe this feeling in the earthly world.

You hear angels singing and beautiful melodies what
seems like instruments, —but can't identify.
The music is so beautifully harmonized, —it's unlike
any music you've ever heard on the earth.

At this moment you are beginning to remember
this place called, "Heaven."

It seems more-and-more familiar to you, —you
know you have been here before.

The deeper you walk into heaven, —you realize this is where
your soul was created, —and everyone's soul was created.
Including all the animals and living creatures of the earth.

You are now given all the divine answers to the questions of life.

You are recognizing it all makes perfect sense.

Your guardian angel brings you to all the loving souls who
lived with you on the earth, —that had passed away.
It is a joyous reunion.

Take a moment to breathe in deeply here.
Exhale slowly, —and imagine what that would be like.

Note what are they saying to you?
What are they showing you?
What radiant visions are you seeing?

You are understanding each soul telepathically, with concise clarity.

Observe no one is ill here.
Everyone looks young and glorious.

Imagine that you are now able to have one request. What would it be?

Remember that this is only a visit.
It is almost time for you to return.

Imagine receiving a warm hug from your loved ones, —ensuring you
that one day you will return to this beautiful, magnificent place.
Until then, —know you are unconditionally care for.

Your awareness and senses are heightened in this paradise.
Your heart is filled with overwhelming joy, love, and support.
You are reassured that God's kingdom is real.

You now have an enormous gratitude for this wonderous journey, —and
for all of God's glorious universe.

Note that you have a deeper sense of peace and joy.

The universe is so infinitely vast and glorious.
You see how God has perfected everything.
He is a mystical being of light that gives all of heaven
an amazing radiance that will be—for eternity.

As you disembark back to earth, —know that God and
all of heaven is always watching over you.
You have a deeper sense of harmony with nature and the world
we live in, —that which mirrors what is said in scripture.

Take a deep breath in, —exhale slowly.

Return to the present time and open your eyes.

At the end of this meditation allow yourself to feel reassured that there is never anything to really be afraid of. God is always protecting us from across the veil. There is infinite love in the universe, —which provides hope, strength, security, and harmony in the world.

Hold on to positive messages and inspirations. Stay focused on positive affirmations, —and feelings of joy, peace, hope, and love that you encountered on this meditation. Understand what really matters most in life.

Take inventory of heaven's gates meditation:

Note how well this meditation worked for you.

Note if there is anything you want to add or take away from this meditation to make you more comfortable.

Was there anything you would want to change for next time such as a longer or shorter version of this kind of meditation?

Remember, —prayer and meditation are an individual practice, —keep it in positive light fostering positive intentions going forward.

14

Country Path Meditation

It is better to know some of the
questions, than all of the answers.
–James Thurber

The purpose of this meditation is to allow yourself to feel refreshed and revitalized. To set positive intentions, and –to take on new projects– that will foster long and short-term goals. Make sure you are in a quiet space, in a dimly lit area. Play soft music with no lyrics. If you wish, –keep healing crystals next to you and diffuse aromatherapy oils.

Take twenty to thirty minutes to enjoy this meditation:

Sit in a comfortable chair or in a cross-legged seat.
Ground yourself to the floor below you.
Place your palms facing down on your lap or
up for more receptivity.
Relax your shoulders.
Close your eyes.

Take a deep breath in through your nose.
Exhale–slowly through your mouth.

Imagine yourself in a wooded area in the country.

You see rolling hills and mountains in the near distance.
It's a spring day and the sun is shining brightly.
You hear baby birds chirping and —its parents
busy flying around to find food.
The trees in the woods are beginning to bloom.
The air is warm and crisp with a gentle wind.
It's a perfect temperature to take a walk on the country path in the woods.

You can invite a loved one or pet to take this walk with you.

As you begin to walk onto the wooded path you notice
multi-colored wildflowers growing in the meadow.
Everything is so bright and alive.

You are feeling energetic and enthusiastic about the spring season.

As you walk into the wooded path take note of the
squirrels and rabbits that are nearby.

Breathe in—new inspiration and joy.
Exhale—any residual tension that has been weighing you down.

Notice sounds of running water, like a stream.
Notice a bench next to a pond with a little waterfall
that flows into a stream along the path.
Take a seat on the bench and just gently breathe
in the glory of that spring day.

In your mind's eye—take note of what else you see.
What sounds you hear in the distance?
And any scents.

Get up from the bench and walk a little further into the woods.
Take note of the beautiful green meadow in the distance.

Walk over toward the meadow and lay down on the grass.
Feel the sun on your face.

Imagine playfully rolling down the hillside with
a loved one or animal in the meadow.
Imagine feeling so overjoyed, —quietly giggling
inside, —how you feel like a child again.

Imagine having no pain or discomfort, —you're just in
complete ecstasy. Having no worries or concerns.

When you look towards the trees, —they are so beautiful with
rich, deep green leaves and an array of magnificent flowers.
As the sunlight reflects off the trees, —you can see
the most magnificent aura around them.

The energy of its aura is felt by all the animals in the woods.
Every animal seems content and happy.

Imagine looking off into the meadow and seeing an apple tree.
It is growing the most inviting apples on it.
You walk over to this apple tree and pick off the most perfect apple.
You taste the apple.
It's the most delicious apple you have ever tasted.
You sit and rest under the apple tree for a while
to take in the beauty of the meadow.

Now imagine yourself running off into the meadow, —feeling
the wind gently blow through your hair.
You are now feeling so free and light.

When you come to the end of the meadow you realize
you are back where you started on this journey.
You are now very relaxed and energized.
You feel confident and strong.
You are ready to take on whatever life has instore for you.

Take a deep breath in.
Exhale slowly.

Open your eyes and start your day.

Take inventory of the country path meditation:

At the end of this meditation—take note of how relaxed you are.

Note how well this meditation worked for you.

Note if there was anything you want to add or to take away from this meditation to make it more comfortable for you?

Note if there are any changes you would want to incorporate going forward?

15

Healing Crystal Cave Meditation

All journeys have secret destinations
of which the traveler is unaware.
–Martin Buber

The purpose of this meditation is to realign the chakras of the body while exploring an imaginary crystal cave on a beach, –which resonates with the chakras of the body. Make sure you are in a quiet space, in a dimly lit area. Play soft music with no lyrics. If you wish, –you can hold or keep healing crystals next to you during the meditation, diffuse a relaxing aromatherapy oil –or blend. To further enhance the experience, –you may also use sensory devices such as a lava lamp or mood lamp.

Take twenty to thirty minutes to enjoy this meditation:

Sit in a comfortable chair or in a cross-legged seat.
Ground yourself to the floor below you.
Place your palms facing down on your lap or
up for more receptivity.
Relax your shoulders.
Close your eyes or lower your eyes to the floor.

Take a deep breath in, then exhale.

Imagine yourself walking along the shore of an island
and you come to the entrance of a mysterious cave.

The entrance is narrow, but very inviting.
It is built around large stones with a distinct glow to them.

As you enter the cave you see glimmering gemstones and minerals
on the walls, —reflecting from the sun's rays by the entrance.

You walk down a staircase made of beautiful, exquisite stones.
The quality of the stones looks rich in texture and warm to the bare foot.
The stones are placed in a pattern leading to other corridors of the cave.

As you walk into the first corridor of the cave, —you notice
a pyramid formation of clear quartz crystals.
They are so magnificent in size and clarity, —you immediately
feel a sense of calm and connection to the divine.

The walls of the cave are made of this magical crystal rock —with
arrows of clear quartz crystals pointing in various directions.
Above the ceiling of the cave, —you notice small peak holes of sunlight
hitting the crystals, —re-energizing them from the heavens above.
You see the aura of the light surround and engulf you with positive,
re-charged energy.

As you walk into the next corridor you see amethyst crystals.
They are embedded into all the walls, floor, and ceiling of the room.
The purple light is magnifying, —leaving you in awe of its beauty.

You feel a sense of complete clarity of the mind and heightened intuition.
You are beginning to feel more alert than you ever felt.
Any pain you were feeling is now completely gone.

Next you notice various blue crystals towards
the entrance of the next corridor.
The entrance is outlined in sapphire crystal hexagon shapes.

Mixed in with turquoise crystals of various shades of color.
Each blue crystals shine radiantly within each
crevasse of the floor and walls of the cave.

You feel enriched with wonder.
You are letting go of all that has been harping on your shoulders.
You feel a greater self-confidence and inspiration.

As you look ahead you see rose quartz crystals in the formation
of what appears to be a bench in the next corridor.
It looks so sublime and inviting.
You walk over to the entrance and peek in the room.
It is the most beautiful room you have ever seen.
It is filled with a mixture of pink and green crystals of varying shades.
The mixture of those colors immediately captivates your eyes.
The emerald stones shine so magnificently and —the pink crystals
shout love, peace, and joy with every breath you take in.

You have an immediate sense of comfort.
The rose quartz crystals align your heart chakra to a state of
complete peace and tranquility unlike you've ever felt before.

You feel completely healed by any past relationships
or grief that has weighed you down.
You heart and lungs are re-energized.
You feel like a child ready to run with all your friends on the playground.

As you walk into the next corridor you see this
immense golden yellow glow within the room.
This glow is so magnificent, —you can sense it
was created with all the glory of God.
It completely irradicates any worries or fears from your inner being.

Your entire body feels the Lord's glory when in this room.
You gain an inner wisdom and —an indescribable re-
balance deep inside the bit of your stomach.

You experience much gratitude for the Lord
and his creations on this earth.
The yellow and gold crystals illuminate the room.
They are masterpieces of radiant light that transcends
into the outer portals of the cave into the blue sky.

Then you step down into a corridor that is interwoven with
orange jasper, tiger's eye, and carnelian crystals and gemstones.

They are so utterly soothing to the eye and put
off a radiance of delightful splendor.
You feel a soothing harmony within you.

The orange aura spirals around the room enveloping
you in utter comfort and content.

You feel an inner strength to cope with any adversity that comes your way.
You feel a deep sense of peace and relaxation.

Now, looking out to what appears to be—the last corridor, —at
a distance you see the gorgeous waters of the Caribbean.

You walk through a room with dazzling red crystals.
The varying shapes and sizes of the red crystals emulate the room.

This color immediately grounds you to the earth providing stability
—as this resonates with your base chakra,
—the foundation of your entire being.

The glorious color of red is so luminous in ruby and red jasper stones.
It roots you to the earth providing a deep sense of understanding
and purpose for your life and —the world within which we live.

As you walk through the end of this glorious cave, —your
body-mind-spirit feels in complete alignment.

You are ready to take on the next chapter in your
life with immense pride and courage.

You step back onto the beach again.

Take a deep breath in, –
exhaling slowly.
Then open your eyes.

Take inventory of the healing crystal cave meditation:

At the end of this meditation- notice how much more confident you feel. Note if it has reduced any fears or anxiety that have been weighing you down.

Note how well this meditation worked for you.

Did you enjoy the experience of exploring a crystal cave?

Note if there is anything you want to add or to take away from this experience.

Are there any changes you would make going forward, –such as a longer or shorter version of this kind of meditation?

Keep in mind meditations can be easily adapted to your preference. The purpose is to make "you" relaxed.

16

Water Cleansing Meditation

Even the smallest act of caring for another
person is like a drop of water, it will make
ripples throughout the entire pond.
-Bryan Matteo

The purpose of the water cleansing meditation is to bring you in harmony with the healing properties of water. Water molecules emulate your spirit and bring restoration to your mind and body. There are many healing properties of aquatic therapy including stimulating circulation, supporting digestion, weight loss, longevity, and–helping with depression and anxiety. Water is nourishing for the body by the absorption of minerals through the pores, –and cleansing for the body in digestion. Two thirds of our body is made up of water, and we cannot live without ingesting it. Make sure you are in a quiet space, in a dimly lit area. Play soft music with no lyrics. If you wish-you can hold or keep healing crystals next to you during the meditation and diffuse a relaxing aromatherapy oil or blend to enhance the experience.

Take twenty to thirty minutes to enjoy this meditation:

Sit in a comfortable chair or in a cross-legged seat.
Ground yourself to the floor below you.

Place your palms facing down on your lap
up for more receptivity.
Relax your shoulders.
Close your eyes.

Imagine walking into a beautiful paradise with endless
magnificent paths leading to the most picturesque
waterways, springs, rivers, and oceans or lakes.
Each waterway emulates gloriously from the sun's rays.

Set an intention of healing through this meditation, —as water
is a unique cleansing property that re-energizes the
mind-body-spirit.

Allow the healing power of water bring positive thoughts
to flow in, —as all negative thoughts flow out.

At any time along this journey, —you may invite someone else in
—to accompany you.

At the entrance to this paradise are tropical plants with
green vines draped around serene trees with flowers of
varying shades of pink, red, orange, yellow and white.

The aromas from the flowers are so pleasant and sublime.

The sand on the pathway in front of you is soft to the touch.
Its so relaxing and tranquil to walk on.

Each pathway branches off in the distance among the brush
and lush gardens.
Each one leads to a special paradise.

One fork along the path sends you into a direction
meeting this marvelous spring of life.

It is a healing grotto that offers a spiritual renewal.
It resonates with heaven's pool of eternal life here on the earth.

The cascading waterfall running into this beautiful
pond is rich with vitamins and minerals.
The water is turquoise in color.
It is completely serene in clarity.

You walk over to this pond and realize it is a natural spring.
The water is so clean.

You touch the water with your hand, —and decide to drink it.
You immediately feel its healing powers.
You begin to realize how much healthier and livelier you feel.

Then you decide to walk into the warm spring and
swim over to the cascading waterfall.
The water feels so refreshing.

You notice there is no fish in this water.
Only colorful gemstones at the base of the pond.
The gems sparkle as the sun's rays reflect-off them.

You feel like you're in heaven.
This spring is completely private, —trees surround
this paradise allowing for complete serenity.

Breathe in, —the freshness of this beautiful spring.
Exhale- any toxins in your body.

Imagine this healing grotto completely refreshing your mind-body-spirit.
Leaving you fresh and renewed.

You step out of the spring.
And work your way towards another waterway.

This time the fork on the path leads to an exquisite beach.
It is looks so tranquil.
The color of the sand is light pink.
The lagoon waters are gently rolling in off the shore.
The color of the water is light blue, —and is so clean and clear.

In the distance you can see dolphins swimming by.

There are lush green plants, moss roses, and orchids growing
along the sides of the lagoon.

In the middle of the beach there is a palm tree.
It is hanging over the shoreline.

There is a comfy looking log under it.
You decide to walk over to the log to sit on it.

Take the time here to take in all that you see, hear, and feel.

Take a deep breath in, —having gratitude
for all that you are experiencing.
Exhale slowly, —releasing all things that have weighed you down.

Now walk towards the pathway again.

Take note of how the mysterious pathway winds ever
to gently in the direction of another paradise.

This waterway is a moving riverbed.
It also has colorful gemstones at the base.
The water is so clean and crisp.
Its color is sublime.
It's the prettiest shade of turquoise you have ever seen.

You walk over to the rivers edge and put your feet in the water.
It is so warm and refreshing.

The stream of the river is moving so gently.

Notice the edge of the riverbank has large smooth rocks to sit and rest on.
You walk over and sit on one of those rocks.

Take a moment here to take in all that you see and hear.

When you are ready—walk a little further up the riverbank.

Notice colorful water-crystals forming from
behind a huge waterfall in the distance.

You decide to walk up the river to get a closer look.
You notice there is more than one waterfall.
Each waterfall has a pool flowing into the next waterfall.
It is absolutely stunning to watch.
The pools of water are a gorgeous shade of blue—and so inviting.

As you get closer you see the magnificent crystals embedded
into the rocks, walls, and base of the pools.

They are shimmering with all kinds of color in the sunlight.
You see amethysts, emeralds, sapphires, pink quartz crystals, clear
quartz crystals, carnelian, topaz, red jasper and more…

All these crystals are beautifully blended into this harmonious place.

You are in awe of this aquatic oasis.

You decide to take a swim in one of the pools of water.
You find it incredibly healing.
Imagine the minerals absorbing into your body—
freeing your mind of life's stresses.
Restoring a more vibrant energetic body.

The water flushes out all unhealthy toxins.

Your spirit is filled with joy.
This oasis of water is so alluring to watch and swim in.
You find it ever so nourishing and enriching to your mind-body-spirit.

Take a deep breath in here.
Exhale slowly.

Know that this oasis is a shrine of miraculous waters.

Your journey is now at its end.
Be aware that you can take this journey again whenever you wish.

When you're ready, return to the present time.
And—open your eyes.

Take inventory of the water cleansing meditation:

Note how well this meditation worked for you.

Note how you feel about water therapy and natural waterways.

Is there anything you want to add or to take away from this meditation experience?

Note if there is anything you would want to change for next time.

17

Affirmations & Insights

The difference between misery and happiness
is what we do with our attention.
-Sharon Salzberg

You are loved more than you know.

Demonstrate compassion and compassion will be returned.

Follow your heart, —it is always speaking to us.

Live life fully.

Don't hold onto anger, —recognize where it came from and free yourself of its source.

Don't allow others to discredit your feelings, —you have intuition for a reason.

React with pure intentions, —only greed will destroy you in the end.

You are stronger than you think, don't let anyone tell you otherwise.

Don't gossip, it discredits your character.

Rid yourself of jealousy, it lowers your light, —you have your own gifts use them with gratitude.

Don't condemn others, —but use judgement wisely in choosing relationships—which is not the same as judging others.

You are responsible for the choices you make, —don't blame others.

Your mind is where you control your thoughts.

Your body is where you control your actions.

Your spirit is where you manifest your most precious gifts.

> *The lord searches every heart and understands every desire and every thought. If you seek him, he will be found by you.*
> *—1 Chronicles 28:9*

The things I know for sure-

God loves each of us divinely.

God shows no favoritism.

Love cannot be forced or coerced.

God is always watching patiently.

God has a divine plan-you are not here by mistake.

Everything we do happens for a reason—including our lessons.

When the lesson is taught, you are all the more accountable for it; —the cross should never be taken for granted.

The Lord will bring light to what is hidden, —he sees our motives.

Everyone has the ability-to succeed; —its why we were born.

When we thrive, we are fulfilling God's purpose for us.

To grow you must learn what suffering is, —it couldn't be otherwise.

We must not only have faith in God, but we must trust in God.

To live a good life is wonderful, —but to live by God's will is profound.

What you do for others, —you do for God.

False intentions do come back to you.

We all make mistakes, —but you do need to take responsibility for those mistakes.

We must learn the core lessons of the earth life now, —or the lessons get harder.

Atonement is not something to be feared, but to be expected, —none of us are perfect, but we need to strive to be better.

We learn from each other and through each other.

Keep in mind our children belong to God, not us, —they too have free will.

Afterword

What inspired me to write this book was my interest in holistic healing practices that I used with patients as a recreational therapist, –and on my own that provided an outlet to reduce stress and anxiety from everyday life.

These guided meditations offer self-help to anyone in need or in practice as optional techniques for healing. The techniques are also provided in audio so they can be practiced alone, offering soothing music and guided imageries to foster relaxation, hope, joy, and inspiration into your

mind-body-spirit.
Please follow me on my webpage at
https://dianecalabrese.com
And-check out my first book
at
BalboaPress Bookstore
https://www.balboapress.com/en/bookstore/
bookdetails/830359-mind-body-spirit-
and-discovering-the-purpose-of-life

Mind, Body, Spirit

And Discovering the

Purpose of life

DIANE CALABRESE

Editorial Reviews of Mind, Body, Spirit and Discovering the Purpose of Life by Diane Calabrese

"This is a concise but comprehensive book which equips the readers with the necessary tools to improve physical, mental, and spiritual health. Diane has carefully picked effective techniques that can easily be learned and practiced in day-to-day life."

Dr. Krishna N. Sharma/Professor, Vice-Chancellor at Victoria University Kampala in Uganda, Bestselling Author, Researcher, and World Record Holder

I Wish I Had This Book 15 Years Ago-
I went through 4 terrible years of depression from 2006 to 2010, chronicled in a book I wrote called HOW I ESCAPED FROM DEPRESSION. Oh, if only I had had this book as a resource, I would have no doubt gotten through it much sooner and much better. My healing was a three-legged stool- body, mind, and spirit - a holistic approach. That's exactly what this book covers, in much detail and helpful suggestions. Oh, Diane, where were you when I needed you. The answer is that it wasn't written yet. Would that it had been. I highly recommend this book for those going through emotional issues or other challenging situations.

Patrick Day, Reverend, President of Pyramid Publishing, author of The Bible Revealed

What a beautiful book! A great go-to for preventative health and healing, packed with a variety of therapeutic modalities, including energy work and sensory techniques, like aromatherapy. What's interesting about this book is that the author incorporates both her stories of healing and her Christian faith, showing that alternative medicine and Christ-centered practice can work hand in hand. I loved hearing about the psychic/spiritual aspects of the author's life as well as her dedication to her therapeutic practices--and the community at large. Her clients are lucky to have her, and readers of this book will find a wealth of resources to guide them.

Jacqueline Henry Moloney is a writer and poet. She is certified in Kundalini Yoga and as a Reiki III practitioner.

"I found Diane's book to be an absolutely fascinating book of holistic techniques! It is very well written and guides the reader step by set using narration, diagrams and beautiful pictures. Also including many inspirational quotes from famous people, this book is not only inspirational but uplifting as well. Whether you are looking to gain in spirituality, or simply relieve stress this book can help. Touching on everything from Chakras, through Yoga, Meditation, Tai Chi and various forms of exercise, this book is a must read!"

Jeff Webber, author of Enimnori books-

"A Must Read! As an indie author myself, this book moved me in many, many ways... From the serene cover to the gentle pictures, this book truly is a find amongst the mind, body, and spirit books in this genre. As an eating disorder provider, I am well aware of the connection between all three! The chapter that truly resonated with me most, as a recovered codependent, is forgiveness and letting go. Easier said than done! This book is a must read for anyone struggling with anxiety and/or has a strong mind body connection and I highly recommend!"

Debra Spector, MS, RDN, CDN Author of– The Things I've Seen People Do With and Without Food

"Fascinating Book-Mind, Body, Spirit and Discovering the Purpose of Life is the most complete collection of mind, body, and spirit techniques in one

book that I have ever seen. Although the book is primarily New Age, it has a strong Christian base. Each chapter covers a different aspect of holistic health. There doesn't seem to be anything left out. I would recommend this book to anyone looking for relief in dealing with the problems of life. Diane Calabrese has had many years of practice as a therapist. Her writing shows that she is a caring soul with the goal of helping others."
Lynn K. Russell, Author of: The Wonder of You, What the Near-Death Experience Tells You About Yourself, and Worpple-

"This book teaches how to take care of our lives physically, mentally, spiritually, and emotionally. It introduces different holistic treatments that help us prevent certain mistakes and illnesses. As humans, we are born with a particular purpose to fulfil, but the problem comes when we don't discover our purpose, and we live according to others' perspectives of us. The book is filled with guidelines that enable us to find the purpose for which we are created. It shows the difference in our individual physical well-being as well as our spiritual well-being. It also portrayed self-healing practices when broken. It is known that our actions result from our thoughts, and the book also helps direct our thoughts to become better humans."
El-limitless Onlinebookclub.org

References & Recommended Readings

Auerbach, Loyd. (2017). *Psychic Dreaming-Dreamworking, Reincarnation, Out-Of-Body Experiences & Clairvoyance*. Llewellyn Publications.

Besteman, Marvin. (2012). *My Journey to Heaven*. Published by Revell, a division of Baker Publishing Co.

Bodine, Echo. (1999). *Echoes of the Soul*. New World Library.

Burke, John. (2015). *Imagine Heaven*. Baker Publishing Group.

Burpo, Todd. (2011). *Heaven is For Real*. Harper Collins Publishing Co.

Calabrese, Diane. (2021). *Mind, Body, Spirit and Discovering the Purpose of Life*. BalboaPress Publishing Co.

Chakra Meditation INFO: Your Chakra Guide (2015). https://www.chakra meditationinfo.com/reiki/reiki-healing/reiki-level-1-guide-to-reiki-practice/

Dougherty, Ned. (2001) *Fast Lane to Heaven*. Hampton Roads Publishing, Inc.

Dyer, Wayne. (2007). *Inspiration Your Ultimate Calling*. Hay House, Inc.

Eadie, Betty J. (1992). *Embraced By the Light*. Golf Leaf Press, Inc.

Hartdegen & Hickey. (1986). *The St. Joseph Edition no. 62 of The New American Bible*. Catholic Book Publishing Co.

Hazel, Raven. (2006). *The Angel Bible*. The Sterling Publishing Group.

https://auraaura.co/aura-colors/

https://www.reiki-for-holistic-health.com

https://www.reikirays.com

https://www.udemy.com/user/drkrishnansharma/

https://www.udemy.com/user/karen-e-wells/

https://www.universalclass.com/

Jankowski, Kelley. (2015). *An Army in Heaven*. Page Publishing Inc.

Kreeft, Peter. (1990). *Everything You Ever Wanted to Know About Heaven-But Never Dreamed of Asking*. Ignatius Press.

Kolbaba, Scott. MD. (2016). *Physician's Untold Stories-Discover the Miracles in Your Life*. CreateSpace Independent Publishing.

Lembo, Margaret Ann. (2016). *Crystal Intentions Oracle, Guidance and Affirmations*. Llewellyn Publications. www.llewellyn.com

Longo, Pat. (2019). *The Gifts Beneath Your Anxiety*. Citadel Press Book, Kensington Publishing Corp.

Martin J. and Romanowski, P. (2009). *Love Beyond Life-The Healing Power of After-Death Communication*. HarperCollins Publishers.

McKenzie, Eleanor. (2009) *The Reiki Bible*. Sterling Publishing, Co.

Myss, Caroline. (2002). *Sacred Contracts*. Harmony Books, NY.

Myss, Caroline. (2017). *Anatomy of the Spirit*. Harmony Books, NY.

Myss, Caroline. (2020). *Intimate Conversations with the Divine*. Hay House Inc.

Neal, Mary. (2012). *To Heaven and Back*. Random House Publishing Co.

Neal, Mary. (2017). *7 Lessons from Heaven*. Random House Publishing Co.

Russo, Kim. (2020). *Your Soul Purpose: Learn How to Access the Light Within*. HarperCollins Publishers.

Schaub, B. and Schaub, R. (2015). *Clinical Meditation Course-Huntington Meditation and Imagery Center*.

Shumsky, Susan. (2013). *The Power of Auras*. Red Wheel/Weiser Publishing Co.

Smith Jones, Susan. (1992) *Choose to Live Peacefully*. Celestial Arts Publishing.

Stephens, Mark. (2020) *Yoga Adjustments Deck*. North Atlantic Books.

Taylor, Ken and Joules. (1999). *Everyday Crystals for a Better Life*. Collins and Brown Limited Publishing Co.

Walsch, Neale D. (2017). *The Wisdom of the Universe-Essential Truths from the Beloved Conversations with God Trilogy*. Random House LLC.

www.pixabay.com/Images

www.pixabay.com/music

www.reiki.org

www.udemy.com

www.youtube.com/reiki

Van Praagh J. and Virtue, D. (2013). *How to Heal a Grieving Heart.* Hay House Inc.

Zukav, Gary. (1989). *The Seat of the Soul.* Simon & Schuster, Inc.

Audiobook accessible at the author's website:
https://dianecalabrese.com
Use code: mantra
To download the audiobook

Printed in the United States
by Baker & Taylor Publisher Services